Gross History

Gross
FACTS About
the American Colonies

BY MIRA VONNE

CAPSTONE PRESS
a capstone imprint

Blazers Books are published by Capstone Press,
1710 Roe Crest Drive, North Mankato, Minnesota 56003
www.mycapstone.com

Library of Congress Cataloging-in-Publication Data
Names: Vonne, Mira, author.
Title: Gross facts about the American colonies / by Mira Vonne.
Description: North Mankato, Minnesota : Blazers, an imprint of Capstone
    Press, 2017. | Series: Gross history | Includes bibliographical references
    and index. | Audience: Grade level 4-6.
Identifiers: LCCN 2016032449| ISBN 9781515741541 (library binding) | ISBN
    9781515741718 (pbk.)| ISBN 9781515741770 (eBook PDF)
Subjects: LCSH: United States—Social life and customs—To 1775—Juvenile
    literature. | United States—Social conditions—17th century—Juvenile
    literature. | United States—Social conditions—18th century—Juvenile
    literature. | United States—History—Colonial period, ca.
    1600-1775—Juvenile literature.
Classification: LCC E162 .V66 2017 | DDC 973.2—dc23
LC record available at https://lccn.loc.gov/2016032449

Editorial Credits
Mandy Robbins, editor; Philippa Jenkins, designer; Wanda Winch, media researcher;
Steve Walker, production specialist

Photo Credits
Bridgeman Images: Alte Pinakothek, Munich, Germany/Bartholome Esteban Murillo, 25, The Stapleton Collection/Private Collection/Adrieen Pietersz van de Venne, 21; Capstone Studio: Karon Dubke, 15; Getty Images: Tria Giovan, 10; Granger, NYC – All rights reserved: Carol M. Highsmith, cover, Sarin Images, 7; Kathy Prenger, 13; National Parks Service/Colonial National Historical Park/Keith Rocco, 17, Sydney E. King, 19, 29; North Wind Picture Archives, 5, 9, 11; Philippa Jenkins, 12; Shutterstock: irin-k, fly design, Kuttelvaserova Stuchelova, 6, Milan M, color splotch design, monkeystock, grunge drip design, Produck, slime bubbles design, Protasov AN, weevil, head lice, parasites, schankz, 22, Thanapun, 19 (rat); White Historic Art/Pamela Patrick White, 23, 27

Essential content terms are **bold** and are defined on the page where they first appear.

Glossary

bloodletting (BLUHD-lett-ing)—a medical treatment thought to cleanse the blood by making the patient bleed

colonist (KAH-luh-nist)—a person who comes from another country and settles in a new area

colony (KAH-luh-nee)—an area that has been settled by people from another country; a colony is ruled by another country

independence (in-di-PEN-duhnss)—freedom from the control of other people or things

nits (NITS)—eggs laid by lice

outhouse (OUT-howss)—an outbuilding with one or more seats above a pit that serves as a toilet

plumbing (PLUM-ing)—the system of water pipes in a building

smallpox (SMAWL-poks)—a disease that spreads easily, causing chills, fever, and pimples that scar

Read More

Lusted, Marcia Amidon. *The Jamestown Colony Disaster: A Cause-and-Effect Investigation*. Cause-and-Effect Disasters. Minneapolis: Lerner Publications, 2017.

Rodgers, Kelly. *The New England Colonies: A Place for Puritans*. Huntington Beach, Calif.: Teacher Created Materials, 2016.

Sherman, Patrice. *How'd They Do That in Colonial America?* How'd They Do That? Hockessin, Del.: Mitchell Lane Publishers, 2010.

Internet Sites

FactHound offers a safe, fun way to find Internet sites related to this book. All of the sites on FactHound have been researched by our staff.

Here's all you do:

Visit *www.facthound.com*

Type in this code: 9781515741541

Super-cool stuff!

Check out projects, games and lots more at
www.capstonekids.com

Critical Thinking Using the Common Core

- The details in this book are gross. What other words can you use to describe colonial living? (Integration of Knowledge and Ideas)

- How do the images add information about the colonies? Describe some of these images. (Craft and Structure)

- Compare colonial living with living today. Would you want to live during the 1600s? Why or why not? (Integration of Knowledge and Ideas)

Index

TABLE OF CONTENTS

A New Home

European **colonists** began coming to America in the 1600s. They wanted a fresh start. What they found wasn't welcoming. Settlers faced harsh weather and gross living conditions. They had to find shelter fast.

colonist—a person who comes from another country and settles in a new area

Some early colonists tied poles and branches together. Families huddled on straw floors with furs or blankets. Others dug cave-like homes. Bugs dug in through the ceiling. Mice, rats, and snakes came in through dirt walls.

6

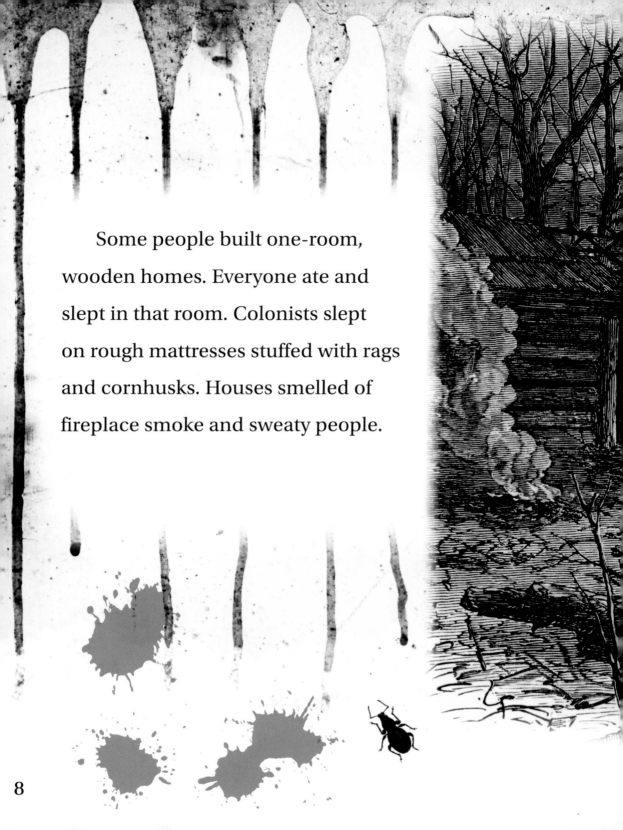

Some people built one-room, wooden homes. Everyone ate and slept in that room. Colonists slept on rough mattresses stuffed with rags and cornhusks. Houses smelled of fireplace smoke and sweaty people.

Gross Grub

At first, colonists ate what they had brought over on the ship. This included dried fruit and vegetables. Sometimes meat became moldy and rotten. Settlers scraped away the mold and ate what was left.

Gross Fact

Colonists' only bread was hardtack, a rock-hard cracker. Beetles often burrowed into the hardtack.

hardtack

11

Bogus Bathrooms

Colonists didn't have indoor **plumbing**. They dug pits near their homes. **Outhouses** were built over the pits. An outhouse seat was a board with a hole in the middle. Waste fell into the pit.

plumbing—the system of water pipes in a building

outhouse—an outbuilding with one or more seats above a pit that serves as a toilet

Gross Fact

There was no toilet paper in colonial America. Colonists used corncobs to clean themselves. They tossed them into the pit after use.

— **corncob**

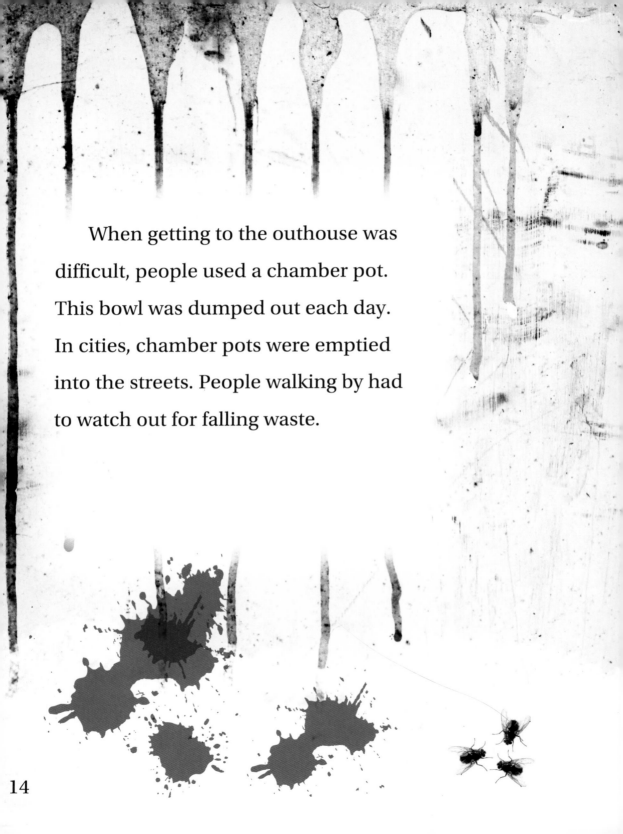

When getting to the outhouse was difficult, people used a chamber pot. This bowl was dumped out each day. In cities, chamber pots were emptied into the streets. People walking by had to watch out for falling waste.

15

Animals added to the waste in the streets. Pigs, cows, and horses wandered through towns leaving droppings behind. Colonists had to watch their steps.

Deadly Diseases

Colonists battled deadly diseases. **Smallpox** was the nastiest. It killed thousands. Victims had blisters break out all over their bodies. Skin died and fell away. Many people who got smallpox died in terrible pain.

smallpox—a disease that spreads easily, causing chills, fever, and pimples that scar

Yellow fever was another common disease. It was spread by mosquitoes. Nearly half of all victims died.

Doctors tried **bloodletting** to cure illnesses. They thought "bad blood" made people sick. Doctors also gave medicines that caused vomiting or diarrhea. They thought releasing bodily fluids took illnesses away.

bloodletting—a medical treatment thought to cleanse the blood by making the patient bleed

Gross Fact

People once believed that the stronger the smell, the better a medicine was. Treatments included tying fish to patients' feet and drinking a broth made of boiled toads.

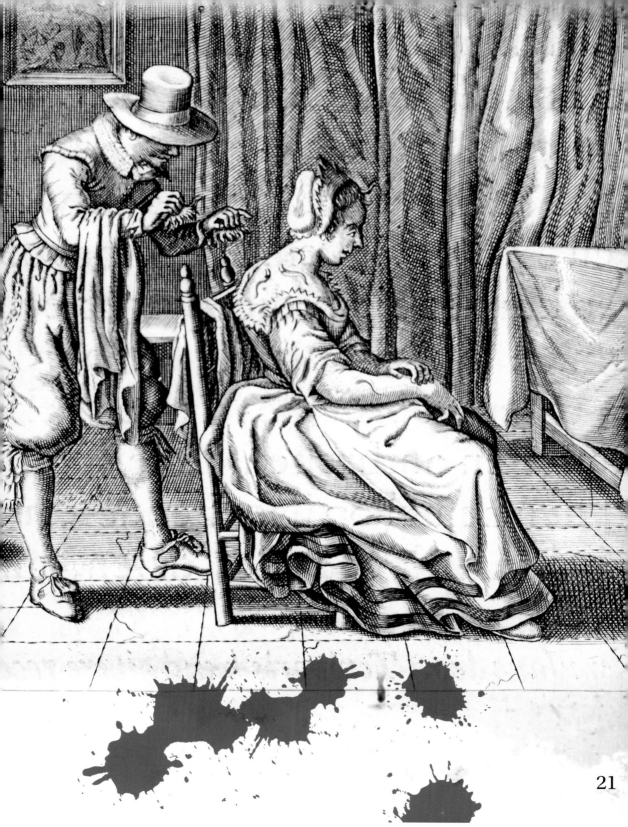

21

What's That Smell?

Colonial people smelled bad. They rarely bathed. Most people believed water was unhealthy. They thought the dirt and sweat caked into their skin protected them from illness.

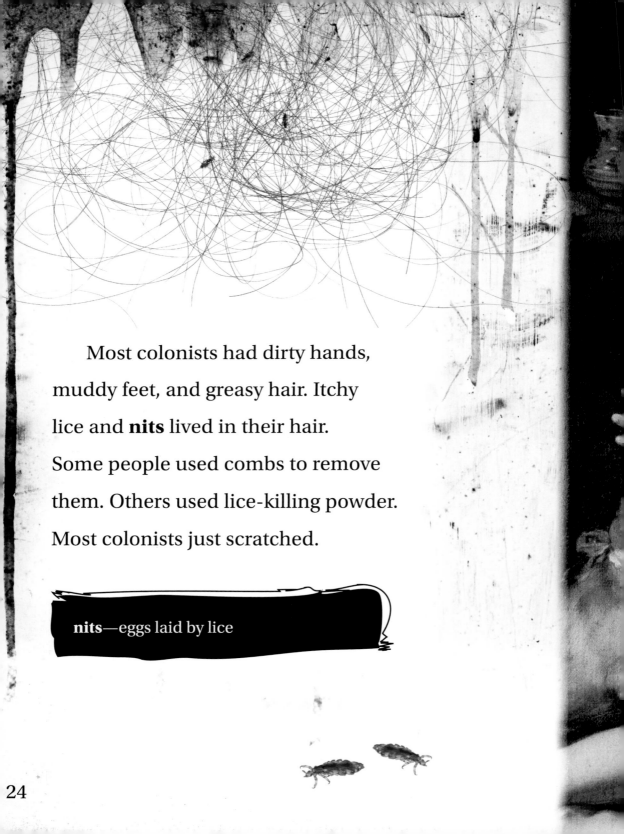

Most colonists had dirty hands, muddy feet, and greasy hair. Itchy lice and **nits** lived in their hair. Some people used combs to remove them. Others used lice-killing powder. Most colonists just scratched.

nits—eggs laid by lice

Colonists tried to clean their clothes. Most people had just two or three outfits. Women hauled water, heated it, and scrubbed by hand. During winter, water froze. People wore dirty clothes until spring.

Changing Times

Life did improve for the colonists. They built bigger houses and learned to grow food. In 1776 the 13 **colonies** declared **independence** from Great Britain. But it would take many years to outgrow the gross colonial times.

independence—freedom from the control of other people or things

colony—an area that has been settled by people from another country; a colony is ruled by another country